A Hull School in Wartime

Kingston High School's Evacuation to Scarborough

by

John D. Hicks

Highgate Publications (Beverley) Limited, 1990

British Library Cataloguing in Publication Data

Hicks, John D. (John David),
 A Hull school in wartime: Kingston High School's evaculation to Scarborough.
 1. Great Britain. Children. Evacuation, 1939-1945
 I. Title
 940.531610941

ISBN 0-948929-29-4

Published by Highgate Publications (Beverley) Ltd.
24 Wylies Road, Beverley, HU17 7AP
Telephone (0482) 866826

Printed and Typeset in 10 on 11pt Plantin by
B.A. Press, 2-4 Newbegin, Lairgate, Beverley, HU17 8EG
Telephone (0482) 882232

ISBN 0-948929-29-4

© J. D. Hicks 1990

Going to the station — the crocodile along Cholmley Street.

In memory of Mary Sheppard (1890 -1990)
Teacher at the Boulevard Secondary School from 1914
Senior Mistress of the Boulevard and Kingston High Schools
1923 -1949

Acknowledgements

Many old Boulevardians and old Kingstonians have shared with me their memories of these days and have lent photographs.

In particular I wish to record thanks to:

Mr F. Cowell	Mrs A. Davidson
Miss J. Dinning	Mrs C. Early
Mr G. Hood	Mr L. Harrison
Mrs A. Headley	Mrs H. Houldey
Miss M. Sheppard	Mr D. Spurgeon
Mr S. Sugarman	Mrs E. Stephenson
Prof C. Taylor	Dr H. Walker
Mrs M. Wilkinson	

Mrs E.J.C. Large for permission to publish 'Evacuadelphi',

The present Headmaster of Kingston School, Mr J.A. Peck, for access to the school records,

and all those too shy to be mentioned in print.

Messrs Walkers of Scarborough took all the photographs of the evacuees at Scarborough and have kindly allowed their reproduction in this book.

The late Mr C. Early took the photograph of the evacuees walking along Cholmley Street.

Kingston High School's Evacuation to Scarborough

August is holiday time and for Les Harrison and many other boys from Hull in 1939 it was just like any other summer. The sun shone, it was fun on the beach at Bridlington, donkeys to ride on, ice cream and candy floss, the shows and the amusements, until that evening when mother saw the *Hull Daily Mail* — 'REOPENING OF HULL SCHOOLS TOMORROW' — and the holiday was over. Like thousands of other boys and girls all over the country he was to find the holiday was over not just for 1939 but for a good many years to come.

Les was a pupil at Kingston High School in Hull. The school itself was new that autumn, having changed its name from the Boulevard Secondary School to coincide with a move into its fine new premises off Pickering Road. Now, with his uniform ready for the new term, he was enjoying the last few days of his summer holiday until his mother saw the notice. Mother brought the family back to Hull in a hurry, and began immediate packing of essential items of clothing from the list supplied by the school months before, and on 1 September, before the proper date for the new school term, there he was with hundreds of other pupils on their way to an unknown destination in a safe area.

Civil Defence plans to protect civilians in case of war had been gradually developed by a government committee which first met in 1924 and by the late thirties detailed plans existed to protect the population should war break out. Information on air raids during the Spanish Civil War had given the government some idea of what modern warfare meant. Detailed planning commenced in Hull in 1938 and one important part of the scheme was to remove young people and mothers with young children from a 'danger zone' consisting of most of the city. The city's Director of Education, R.C. Moore, put out his plans in good time. His education department had been issuing instructions throughout that significant year.

In February 1939 the Headmaster of the Boulevard Secondary School, Dr W. Cameron Walker, was in communication with the education department as his staff could not get to Villa Place School in time for a 4.30 p.m. meeting of the anti-gas course being run for teachers. As both he and his Head of Physics, Clifford Early, were being trained as instructors, he wanted permission to run his own course for Boulevard staff after the school Hobbies Exhibition and Prize Distribution at Easter. This lack of real understanding of what threatened the civil population if war was declared, and the great urgency to have as much preparation completed as possible, was not unusual at this time with many people still expecting there to be no war.

In March 1939 maps were published showing the areas whose schools would be evacuated, as a school was to be the evacuation unit. The Boulevard School was one of those to be evacuated to a safe area should war be threatened.

Over 500 parents attended a meeting at the school on March 22 1939 and both school halls had to be used. Information was to be given out on the proposed plan for evacuation. Parents not surprisingly had many questions to ask and not all could be answered:

> Having once accepted an evacuation place for a pupil, could a parent change her mind?
>
> Can scholarships be transferred where parents have a relative to send a child to for the war?
>
> Who pays for evacuation? — (This became quite an issue later.)
>
> Are details of the evacuation area available? (This questioner seemed to be looking for political motives behind the scheme.)
>
> Will all schools close at the outbreak of war?
>
> What would happen to children whose parents were killed in an air raid?
>
> Should the signing of the form depend on the reactions of the child to the idea of going away from its parents?
>
> What arrangements have been made for the education of children not evacuated?
>
> Could parents volunteer to come and look after children?

Cameron Walker noted that there was considerable confidence in the staff's ability to look after the children but assurances were needed that the school would be kept together. Parents were very concerned that details of next-of-kin were filed away. Parents were very uneasy about the non-return of children to relatives if these details were not known. Concern was expressed at using the school as the assembly station and many would have preferred some other and safer location. Not all the questions could be answered, even though the Headmaster had been supplied with a sheet entitled 'Points for Speech at Parents' meetings'.

In May 1939 instructions for the emergency scheme for evacuation were published. It was hoped to give three warnings of impending action. The first was so that all concerned could prepare, the second to be prepared to move at 24 hours notice, and the final notice was to be a time and date. It was even arranged to publish a special edition of the *Hull Daily Mail* with evacuation arrangements if necessary.

Boulevard pupils were already in groups under a member of staff or adult helper and they now knew they would assemble at school at 11.00 a.m. and leave Hull Paragon by train at 1.30 pm on whatever day was chosen.

There was a special Air Raid Precautions (ARP) meeting at school on 10 July at 4.00 p.m. On this occasion final lists were made of pupils to be evacuated and those who would remain in the care of their parents. Everyone, including staff and helpers, had to give their holiday addresses in case they were needed at short notice. About 350 pupils were allocated to groups and all that was needed was a date and a location. The authorities were not giving advance information about reception areas but Cameron Walker had been long enough in Hull to have gained friends and it was a parent who gave him advance information and the chance to pay a visit to Scarborough and see the billeting officer before war was declared.

The Boulevardian (July 1939) said:
> After nearly half a century in the Boulevard, the School has removed into the new building, the Kingston High School. This has been the last term of those many years during which we have looked forward to the new School. Every member of the staff and every pupil can enter the Pickering Road building with feelings only of confident anticipation ...

but that was not to be.

William Cameron Walker was the Headmaster who will always be remembered in association with the early days of Kingston High School. Born in the West Riding, and with strong family connections with the Moravian community at Fulneck, he attended Hanson School, Bradford, and went on to study chemistry at London University. After obtaining a first class B.Sc. in 1922, he proceeded to M.Sc. and A.K.C., and finally Ph.D in 1937. He taught at Minchenden Grammar School, Enfield, for 14 years, including 9 years as Head of Science, before being appointed Headmaster from January 1938 at the age of 43. Cameron Walker was always noted as a cautious administrator and he tackled the logistics of removing his school across the city with some cunning. He arranged for every pupil to be issued with all new books for the September term before the holidays started, thus ensuring that there would be no confusion at the beginning of term and his removal problems would be lessened. This simple tactic became both a strength and a weakness when the new building was not occupied as expected.

The sudden announcement of evacuation caught a number of people unprepared. Two members of staff were on their honeymoons and had to bring their new wives back to Hull only to find, most unusually, their newly married state included having thrust upon them an immediate cluster of children. In most marriages there is time to get *gradually* adjusted to the

patter of tiny feet but not for Miles Lerner or Burt Gooderham and their wives. Not all children managed to be back in Hull by 11.00 am on Friday morning and there was to be a considerable number who arrived several days or even weeks late in Scarborough. Geraldine Rodgers was to write shortly after arrival:
> The helpers at the station were all too busy for words. Everyone was overworked, children were excited and in some cases frightened. We were packed into trains and set off to 'we didn't know where'. Would it be a house or a tent? What would it be like?

With thoughts like that, Scarborough might have been an anti-climax. When the children knew their destination there was great delight with visions of a never-ending seaside holiday in the months to come. They had with them their school books, of course, but such matters as schoolwork were not in everyone's mind in the excitement of boarding the special train. As no educational arrangements had yet been made, their expectations were largely met for several weeks. The sun shone, the phony war showed no signs of changing and life was not too unpleasant beside the sea.

On arrival the various parties ended up in their billets. The youngest boys were with the Headmaster in the Prince of Wales Hotel on the front, with large parties of boys in the Adelphi, Windsor and Holbeck Hotels, and most of the girls in the Astoria Hotel under Miss Phillips. Smaller groups of boys or girls went into boarding houses and hotels along Grosvenor Crescent, Esplanade Gardens and Albion Road, with Miss Sheppard originally with the older girls at billet no. 2. In the old Boulevard School building boys were on the ground floor and girls upstairs, with separate accommodation for male and female staff. These arrangements had even been part of the planning for the new Kingston High School building. So it is not surprising that throughout the evacuation there were never to be boys and girls (or male and female staff other than married couples) sleeping at the same location. The proprieties were to be preserved even in wartime. It was only with the problem set as a result of children returning to Hull that the evacuated school had to have mixed classes. Later, in Scarborough, there were even mixed swimming classes which caused a great deal of unease amongst staff. Geraldine wrote:
> At last we arrived. Hot, tired and breathless, we were taken to our rooms via the lift. Bewildered? We had never even dreamt of this. We unpacked our haversacks, straightened our clothes, and began to get ready for our life in our new home.... What a life! I don't think any girl has enjoyed herself as much, without her parents, as I have done!

Cameron Walker's official report went:
> The evacuation occurred without a hitch on 1 September when 147 boys, 164 girls, 33 staff and 25 helpers were transferred to Scarborough — in all 311 pupils and 58 adults, complete with

> haversacks, suit cases, gas masks and mackintoshes — surely the strangest seaside party any of us had ever experienced. That night we were all safely under cover in some thirteen hotel or boarding house billets...

The suddenness of the evacuation caught the Scarborough authorities incompletely prepared at the height of the summer season and the children were often crowded as many as ten to a bedroom for the first few nights until rooms became available. At least they were spared the problem of becoming unwelcome guests in private houses, which was the lot of some of the London evacuees in the Scalby area.

One unhappy host wrote:

> Dear Sir,
>
> I am going home. Please remove the two boys in my care. We came here to retire for peace and quiet, and now this blight has come.

The Prince of Wales considered itself superior to its neighbours and still had its regular summer visitors there when, on the instructions of the billeting officer, Dr Walker arrived with about 35 small boys, each carrying his personal luggage. The hotel somewhat grudgingly packed them in, several to a room, and the boys proceeded to enjoy the high life. The sea was just across the road, friends nearby, and the experience of staying in a big hotel something new and worth writing home about. Boys, being curious, soon found out that late at night other guests put their shoes outside their bedroom doors and mysteriously they became clean and newly polished overnight. The boys tried this idea, but 35 extra pairs of shoes to clean, a maximum payment from the government for room and three full meals daily of just 6/- a week was too much for the Prince of Wales and the boys were moved to less exciting premises.

There was a sudden insight into the dangers and perils of war and evacuation in particular when, about 6.00 am on the very first morning in Scarborough, a great explosion brought terror to one of the hotels. It was not the Germans shelling Scarborough again as they had in the First World War, just a teacher's wife, Mrs Hought, trying to make herself an early morning cup of tea with an unaccustomed geyser.

Dennis Spurgeon, a first-year boy, wrote in the school magazine:

> I live in a very cosy billet with ten other boys... It is quite near the sea-front at a spot where, in summer, people would pay much money to stay. The owner of the house is Mrs Richardson, a kind lady, who does not like too much noise.

Poor Mrs Richardson, 11 noisy eleven-year-olds and her not liking 'too much noise'.

Our writer continued:

> Now there are many activities I like at 'Kingsclere'. We have many

Photograph of girls outside the Astoria Hotel, Scarborough.

Back row (left to right) Joan Mitchell, Mary Johnson, Geraldine Rodgers, —, —, Margory Saynor, —, —, Monica Gibson, —, —, Joyce Holland, Joyce Hams, —, Bill, —, —, Joan Norris, —, —, Mary Pretty, Betty Whitelam, —, —, Joan Dinning, —, —, Mary Frank, —,
Second row (left to right) Freda Gerstein, Nellie Soulsby, —, Mary Potts, —, Mary Fish, Ivy Longley, —, —, —, —, —, —,
Audrey Hole, Janette Cousins, Alice Pedder.
Third row (left to right) —, —, —, —, —, —, Pauline Fletcher, —, —, —, —, —, Rosabel Doonan, Marjorie Berry, Mary Bousfield.
Seated (from the left) Miss Dean, Miss Upex, Miss Pyrah, Miss Younghughes, Miss Hanby, Miss Sheppard, 4 members of the Truefitt family, then the parent helpers.

Front row (left to right) —, —, —, Ann Sugarman, —, —, —, —, —, —, Monica Oxtoby, Mavis Brown.

Helpers and Staff at the Astoria Hotel
Front row seated (left to right) Miss Pyrah, Miss Sheppard with VIM, Miss Upex.
Second row (left to right) Miss Dean, Miss Younghughes, Miss Hanby.

> good games ... What I enjoy most of all, though, is a good bath and a good wash; that's the finest thing of all!

Mrs Richardson must have been just unlucky, boarding perhaps the only schoolboy ever to leave Hull who yearned for expensive hot water:

> I dislike however washing-up and 'slipper'. Washing up is boring and most people will agree with me. 'Slipper' hurts too much and that is why I do not like it. We have a pet parrot which talks. It can even sing. In the morning it says 'Good-morning!' And at night it says 'Good-night!' When we wash up it tells us to hurry up.
>
> We cannot do as we like because we are not in our real homes but we have a good time and can enjoy ourselves.

The girls in the Astoria numbered between a 100 and 130 at different times. This was the main mistresses' base and, when in 1940 the girls were nearly all moved there, Miss Mary Sheppard (Senior Mistress) reigned supreme. Miss Sheppard had joined the school staff in September 1914 and had been in charge of the girls since 1923. She was the senior member of staff at Scarborough once the Headmaster was called back to Hull and was a powerful influence on both boys and girls, though the boys were nominally under the Senior Master, Mr Arthur C. Goodwin, who had his wife and two sons with him. As soon as the girls moved in, the Astoria was given over entirely to them and nearly all the staff left. There was just Bill, the porter and odd job man, left with the owners, Mr and Mrs Truefitt and their family. The Truefitts also owned the Adelphi Hotel, which was packed with boys. The staff left because the government payment was not designed to cover the cost of servants and the girls and staff would have to do most of the work in the hotel. Bill immediately offered to do the cooking and he became the mainstay of the Astoria mistresses. However, the staff were responsible for breakfast, organising the washing up and cleaning as well as the problem of keeping the children clean, tidy and with clothing repairs done promptly.

Pupils noted:

> When I used to stand in awe of Miss — I certainly never dreamt she would serve my meals, but now it does not seem out of place at all.
>
> It is very hard to attend lessons when one has seen the teacher performing queer antics at a concert or toiling to stop a burst pipe, dressed up to the ears in waterproofs, but it does make the mistresses seem more human.

They even had time to become rather smug about things as in this essay by C. E. Smith of Va — 'For and Against Evacuation':

> Evacuation is a serious business, for there is yet time for air-raids, and when they do come, woe betide the poor children who, for shelter, cling to mother's apron strings in the middle of a burning city.

Mr E. J. C. Large, Head of English and a noted versifier, put their experiences into a long poem he called, 'Evacuadelphi; or War at the Seaside'. It starts with:

> Arrival and Welcome
> Dear Mrs Truefitt; you'll remember
> How, one late evening last September,
> City scallywags in droves,
> Louts and stiffs and scruffs and coves,
> Came and stood on your front flags,
> Dangling little carrier bags.
>
> Your guests turned green, then pale, then red,
> Gave one despairing glance and fled;
> Screamed as they banged their suit-case lids: -
> 'The blessed place is full of Kids!'
>
> But your kind welcome changed distress
> To seven months of happiness.

More later.

Education at Scarborough was a matter for the North Riding Education Committee. After a delay of several weeks the Kingston pupils were allowed to use the nearby Scarborough High School for Boys, on afternoons only. This hardly provided for the needs of a school that prided itself on its examination results so morning classes were arranged in odd corners of billets, with most occurring in the larger hotels. The available rooms were all too small for classes so smaller units had to be improvised and there was correspondence between the Headmaster and his Head of Physics about the desirability of classes going on outside visits to such places as the harbour.

Sharing premises had other problems too. Mistresses noticed that girls on first entering a classroom always opened their desks. This was puzzling as no Kingston books were stored in the desks. Miss Sheppard wrote recently:

> Suddenly and to my horror, the fact arose that they were writing letters to each other and making arrangements to meet after school in the Valley Gardens. It was useless to tackle individuals so the Staff and I took a crocodile of all the girls straight home after school, across the Bridge, under which the thwarted young men were waiting for their specials. I laugh now as I remember the girls' faces as they peered helplessly over the bridge.

Cameron Walker officially recorded:

> The first three weeks were spent mainly out of doors and in becoming used to boarding school conditions. Fatigue duties were allocated and each billet organised as a separate unit in a way best suited to the particular building and the age of the pupils in it. In the meantime plans were prepared for beginning work in the Scarborough Boys' High School. 120 girls and boys from West Hartlepool Secondary Schools and their teachers were

incorporated into our School and began work with us on the afternoon of 25th September. Soon afterwards we were able to supplement the afternoon lessons in the school by two morning lessons in the billets, thus bringing our working day up to practically normal.

...By the end of September we had a flourishing school of nearly 450 children working on a normal timetable on all the subjects of the curriculum.

There were problems still to be faced, but at first there was a firm belief that the evacuation would not be for long, and that they would enjoy themselves as much as possible under these strange and exciting circumstances.

The great laundry problem became a major issue at Scarborough. When the children first moved into the hotels and boarding houses it was immediately obvious that these premises were not equipped to handle visitors' laundry. Pupils from other schools billeted in private houses had no such problems and their hosts did their laundry. The hotels were used to bedding and towels but the masses of socks, shirts and tunics that several hundred children soil in a week were far beyond the facilities of the various premises. Kingston High children were advised either to send a parcel home each week or pay for it to be done by a Scarborough laundry. Most parents accepted this ruling and there were very few pupils having problems, but some families were finding the cost of evacuation excessive and looked for economies.

One mother wrote to the Director of Education:
> Another thing we should like to point out is the washing, which is sent home at a cost of about 6d and returned later at the same amount. If this was not sent home we should be expected to pay the laundry bill, why?

Miss Sheppard wrote to Dr Walker:
> I am sorry to trouble you in a small matter but the boys are deluging me with cuttings from the *Mail* stating that Alderman Fryer says the billeting allowance covers laundry charges. In one case a boy with a maintenance grant and a liberal supply of pocket money states that his father has told him to refuse to pay laundry.

The Headmaster replied:
> Dear Sir,
>
> I understand that he received 6d on Saturday. Of this he has spent 2d on sweets; he owed 1d to another boy and he has 3d left with which to pay postage for his clothing to be sent home for washing.
>
> Postage will be not less than 6d.
>
> Yours truly,
> W. Cameron Walker

Entertainment at the Astoria Hotel with Miss Dean, Miss Sheppard, Miss Phillips, Miss Upex, and Miss Pyrah.

After Alderman Fryer had spoken, the official position was known, but it did not solve the problem in the hotels and must have been a major consideration when the hotels began to want the evacuees out.

In September, when all the school staff were at Scarborough and only about 400 children (out of a possible 600), there were few problems with out-of-school supervision. Staff willingly gave time on an evening to organise entertainment and deal with routine welfare. Once part-time schooling started in Hull at the Newland High School building in November, a large part of the staff were withdrawn to Hull and there was a dramatic increase in the work load at Scarborough. Staff who were teaching full-time and had lesson preparation and marking to do out of school had little time to supervise children. Many continued to try but by Christmas the strain was beginning to show.

Letters like this did not help:
> We understand our boy has not been wearing his undervests and were afraid of something like this occurring. Should he still be going without them will you please enforce the wearing of them...

Or the straightforward blackmail:
> When I arranged for her to be evacuated I was given to understand that she would be able to be billeted with a friend of mine and one of the helpers at one of your billets. She is a very sensitive child probably due to being an only one, and while I have always tried not to fuss or be too indulgent I am afraid the time has come when she will have to be moved if possible or I shall be reluctantly compelled to have her back.

Another gem:
> I was annoyed and perturbed when he arrived minus gas mask and to hear that he had been without a mask for about two weeks. In my opinion every scholar whether in an evacuated area or not should be given weekly instruction and drill in the care and use of the respirator.

The Scarborough authorities refused to supply replacement respirators to any evacuees and Dr Walker was able to reply:
> I can take no responsibility for the Scarborough Authority if they do not feel disposed to supply careless evacuees with new respirators. The teachers are doing all in their power under difficult circumstances to look after the boys and I feel that the boys at any rate should do their part in looking after their own property.

One staff member wrote to Dr Walker:
> If it is possible, I wish to return to Hull permanently after Christmas. I do not mind who takes my work here, and I am willing to sacrifice the advantages of taking Matric and Higher Certificate forms for the sake of rest and peace.

And again:
> Immediately after our wedding we had to come to this boarding house cum boarding school existence, and quite willingly I must say, at the time. I feel that my wife and I are entitled to taste home life which, at present, seems to be put off indefinitely. We have a house in Hull in which we have never lived ... and we are faced with the prospect of the house going to ruin before we have ever lived in it.

His problem was solved when a few months later his call-up papers arrived.

Clifford Early (Head of Physics) wrote to Cameron Walker:
> My first reaction was to write 'To blazes with you and your blithering infant — take him away if you like.' but Miss Sheppard smoothed me over and I have watered it down.

There are always two sides to every question:
> Mr Hopkinson received me at the entrance. I talked to him a few minutes about the boys and their lessons. He then said, 'Shall I show you the bedroom?' I replied, 'Well really one does not know what to do. I don't know whether to let him stay here or take him home with me.' He then replied, 'If you feel like that, the best thing to do is to take the bull by the horns and take him home, as I do not want any more boys to be unsettled.' And with that I brought him home. I know full well teachers' nerves and patience must be almost exhausted, and so are mothers'.

Cameron Walker put in his annual report to parents:
> And what a blessed peace descended upon those billets at 7.30! If ever I needed further proof of the real value of homework I found it in Scarborough. For one brief hour the staff were able to relax and to enjoy peace of mind and spirit. I know now why parents, in the main, are unanimous in favour of homework.

And later:
> It goes without saying that excuses for not doing homework have been most difficult to find.

However, there were other things going on at night that not even Cameron Walker envisaged. These extracts are from the school magazine:

NINE THIRTY AND AFTER, AT THE ADELPHI
> At 9.30 or sometimes a little later, the prefects are asked to tell the other boys that it is bed-time. The prefects' announcement is greeted by loud yells of protest but there is generally little argument, and the boys move upstairs...

BEDROOM SILENCE 'Hark! I hear horses.' *Macbeth*
> At 10.00pm all lights should be out and prefects take a look round to see that all is in order. Often a prefect hears sinister scrapings and light footsteps. He knows what this means. There's a raid! He

runs towards the noise which ceases as soon as he is spotted. Silence falls as if by magic. On entering the rooms in the 'affected area', he finds everyone in bed, blissfully sleeping...

But another phase of the night-life at the Adelphi begins at about 11.30. Those who do not know the Adelphi and its inmates think that faint murmurings, crunches and pops, coming from nowhere in particular, are signs of the place being haunted. But anyone 'in the know' guesses that there is a feed in progress. The masters do not hear this because it is warmer in bed than out. The culprits, however, are punished. They spend an uncomfortable night among crumbs. But eventually sleep comes even to them and 'the rest is silence'.

H. K. class Va

[Assurance is given that, as soon as the warmer weather comes, the matter will be dealt with. H.K.'s disclosures will prove valuable documentary evidence. -Ed]

'Evacuadelphi' had something to say about certain individuals:

The Motley Crew

Of course, I can't in full transcribe
The names of all that motley tribe :-
Geoffrey and Joe with all their games,
And Stanley with his head in flames;
Dukes and Piercy, Fitton, Potts,
Harper, Green and Tiger Watts;
Grimwood, skilled with billiard ball,
"Ping-pong Smith', and Trip the tall;
Hewitt, Greenwood, Oates and Tate
With all his illnesses; the great
Harbord, the Smiths both H and C,
And Plaxton, always late for tea.

Latus's never-ending smiles,
Kenmure and his pudding – wiles;
Williams, as active as a hare,
Brabb, Hunter, Marshall — all were there.

Barker's studious demeanour,
And Fraser, washed but not much cleaner;
Taylor, straining both his ears
To catch the music of the spheres,
And leaning up against the wall,
Near the wireless in the hall;
And Goodwin, quietest of all.

Finestein, solid, deep and true,
Always wondering what to do,

Mrs Trufitt and the Astoria Hotel girls with Miss Phillips and Dr Walker on the back row. Who is the one boy near the centre?

Rolling out of bed at night,
Nor getting back without a light;
Mr Goodwin, Head of Billet,
And Mrs Goodwin, through whose skill it
Was that boys who squirmed with pain,
(Collywobbles, muscle-strain,
And all the aches and ills there be
From whooping-cough to housemaid's knee)
Speedily swallowed certain cures
And smiled on falling temperatures.

Hodgson, Wright and Codd and Scruton;
Vinegrad with his perfect suit on,
Suave, trim, easy on the eye
With Nature's own simplicity;
Kersh, dark and straight. Beware! beware!!
His flashing eyes, his gleaming hair!
Baker with chestnut waves and curls,
The sheer despair of all the girls,
Or (if you would prefer it) lasses,
Who faint in hundreds as he passes;
Wilkinson, independent, free,
Who jumped full-clothed into the sea
And saved a life — for one-and-three!

Dean, proud of loose, unlovely 'bags',
The waggiest of all the wags;
And the dark-haired charm of Nancy,
Who captured everybody's fancy;
Mr and Mrs Arthur Scott,
And me, the queerest of the lot;
And many others, whom to mention
Would put a strain on your attention.

Schoolboys, especially grammar schoolboys, sometimes think they are a good deal more clever than they are. Letters were sent home to create an effect and were not always intended to be taken literally. One boy wanted to return home. He used considerable skill in writing to his parents but they, much dismayed at conditions, sent the bundle to the Headmaster stating that they were removing their boy to safety in Hull and,

> Hoping this letter will be the means of helping you to get 'Fair Play' and 'Justice' for those other boys of yours who are having to endure the same as our son.

Some samples from these doleful letters:

> Thank you for the parcel last week-end and then the one this week. The food inside just does for me... I would like to come home to

stay if possible soon... We are all keeping well here... P.S. We have never seen a fire.

I was disappointed when you said I could not come home for good... The food is gradually getting worse. On Friday we had a fire but never again. [His hotel had central heating.] Another thing is that when we go into the bedroom for some books or anything else we cannot have the light on. I would very much like to come home. In the morning we have a burnt paste called porridge. About a week ago several mines were exploded at north side and the explosions shattered several windows here. Here at the billet we get a bath approximately every fortnight. [The head noted: At least every week — can have a shower every night.] Also another new thing is that we have to buy our own jam [not true] from now on. These are only a few of the reasons that make me want to come home.

If possible I shall be coming home a week on Saturday... This will be a good job. Thank you for the food you sent me yesterday. Everything was all right. I do not think I shall be needing any more from now on as I have three boxes of biscuits.

Some boys took their demands to return home to extremes and one started a major row in Hull Council and nearly caused his headmaster to be censured for giving out false information. Miss Sheppard spoke to all the children telling them that they were expected to remain at Scarborough but wanting to know if any intended going home should Kingston High School open. This boy wrote home claiming that, if he didn't return home immediately, he would not be able to attend the new Kingston High School when it opened. He was writing more than four months before the building did open. His letter was quoted in the *Hull Daily Mail* on 9 November under the heading 'A school problem solved':

    All the replies must be in by Thursday. Most of the boys are saying they want to go home but I am leaving it for you to decide.

The Chairman of the Education Committee, Alderman Fryer (an old boy of the school), spoke without checking first and said, 'It is very unsatisfactory that this should have taken place ... and I believe the Headmaster of the Kingston High School did ask the children evacuated at Scarborough to write to their parents to ask whether they wanted them to come home or not. It is contrary to our instructions given out. We shall take steps to see that none of the children are influenced to any extent by that.'

Alderman Fred Holmes: 'It is about time this Council told these Headmasters where they get off.' (Hear, hear). He then asked for an assurance that disciplinary action should be taken. However, there was no truth in the story whatever and the Chairman and Director of Education combined to stop Miss Sheppard refuting these allegations in a letter to the

Mail. No apology is recorded as having been made and the boy who started this scare cannot now be identified.

Miss Sheppard can have the last word through the letter she sent to Cameron Walker:

> I hope you are not at all disturbed by the Committee. They are all so profoundly in the dark about the work that is being done that it is useless to enlighten them. I thought Alderman Fryer was more clear sighted though.

Parents were expected to make a contribution to the cost of looking after their children under evacuation. This did not occur at first and some parents seemed to have got into the habit of expecting everything to be free. There was a considerable correspondence with the Headmaster about fees. Six shillings and later 7s 6d a week was a great deal of money for some families to pay out for just one child, especially if they had more than one child away from home, and the total cost could be more than the family income after rent had been paid. Some children were withdrawn for just this reason, with some parents having to make the difficult choice of which child to withdraw and which to leave in safety. There was another side to this, however. All children at Kingston High School had passed the special places examination and parents were entitled to financial assistance according to income. One parent was happily pocketing a grant of several pounds a year and refusing to make any contribution towards the cost of a child at Scarborough.

A different picture is revealed through figures published in the *Hull Daily Mail* which showed that, of 9,000 Hull school children who might be subject to payment, on a first investigation 6,000 were to be free. Of the remainder, 1,000 had agreed to pay the weekly fee of six shillings. There had been 600 appeals against assessments and 500 had, as a result of further information, been reduced. This left only about 100 in dispute though it would appear that some families had not made a sufficiently strong application and were still being assessed unreasonably. There are many letters on file showing the problem as parents saw it:

> The reason is that the amount fixed by the Evacuation Committee is more than I can afford. I am sorry to do this but £2 18s 5d does not go very far with a wife and three children to provide for.
>
> I have received notice from the Evacuation Authority that I must pay a weekly sum of 3/- for each of my three children out of my weekly income of £2 7s 7d.
>
> I am a police constable, and I have since the commencement of the war suffered a reduction in wages and I find it quite impossible to carry on living at what would be above my income.
>
> Circumstances compel me to take this course because I cannot afford to pay the amount they have assessed me to pay for my two children at present evacuated, it is 12/- per week.

> Mam and I have further considered the matter of you coming home and decided that we cannot afford to keep you away. It is costing too much.

> I regret to say we cannot see our way clear of sending her as the expense is more than we can at present afford.

The winter of 1939-40 was one of the worst for many years. There were heavy falls of snow, it was very cold, and, while the children enjoyed their leisure outside, there were serious problems for the teachers to contend with. The Scarborough hotels and boarding houses were mainly for summer visitors, and, though the typical English summer often requires some heating in hotels, none of the buildings occupied by the school was normally fully occupied all the winter. There were not merely serious problems of heating; even the plumbing could not be relied on. In the girls' base at the Astoria Hotel there were constant problems thawing out the water pipes. After considerable exertions the girls would manage a morning wash, only to find on their return after school that the whole thawing-out process had to start again. This caused many incidents still remembered today, like that evening when a pipe burst on the top floor and the water ran through four floors to the basement. The boys of the school choir arrived for their weekly rehearsal only to find Miss Upex, with the other female staff, mopping up instead of being ready for the practice. The ladies could not find the stop tap and were gradually losing the battle as the basement filled with water. One girl was going round collecting face cloths to use for mopping up! Once the boys and the men arrived, the stop tap was found by Clifford Early under several feet of snow, the mopping up went ahead — and presumably the choir practice started a little later.

By this time Cameron Walker was making regular visits by car or train to Scarborough despite the weather:

> 13.2.40
>
> Dear Miss Sheppard,
>   Apart from a few uncomfortable skids and a queer feeling inside, the journey home was quite uneventful and took little longer than usual...
>
>   W. Cameron Walker

A poem, 'Il Penseroso', in the school magazine, painted a vivid picture of wintery conditions:

> It's cold — it's freezing hard — it blows:
> The pipes won't run — it's dark — it snows;
> We'll all be here till crack of doom,
> For generations — till our tomb.
> We've chilblains — sneezes, coughs and sniffs;
> We've lost our hats over the cliffs.
> The ducks are frozen in the pool —

> We should have skis to go to school.
> The black-out curtains won't fit tight —
> We can't have our electric light.
> We have to wash in china mugs
> With water passed around in jugs.
> Oh yes! we're plentifully fed,
> We know we have a nice warm bed.
> Oh no! our play-room's never chill;
> It's true we're cared for when we're ill;
> We do not wish to make the best
> Of work and play and food and rest:
> For Scarborough is a bitter pill;
> We want to grumble — and we will.
>
>   Anon

L'Allegro showed that even problems had their lighter moments:

> Floods of icy water, falling
> Through three floors on skin-drenched staff;
> Mops and buckets in profusion —
> Sights to make the dourest laugh!
>
> Steaming pails of soapy water
> Round a small gas-fire at night,
> Changing pale-grey necks and faces
> Into dreams of sheer delight.
>
> Keep the old school marching onward;
> Never change its cheery face;
> In a week — a month — or next year —
> We'll be there to claim our place.
>
>   Anon

Health problems were a constant threat to the well-being of the evacuees. There were few married staff, and even fewer had experience of looking after children full-time. Minor injuries were constantly being reported and pupils taken to the local hospital for examination:

> ... I was rather worried as he had a very bad cold and a very bad throat. I got him a tonic made up as soon as I arrived in Scarborough. — A parent on a visit.

> You will perhaps be wondering not hearing from me but I have been waiting to see if Richard developed any sign of scabies. I sincerely hope there have been no further cases in the billet. — Letter to Headmaster.

> Dear Dr Walker,
> I have to report that the doctor has been called in to see three boys and has found them suffering from scabies. They have gone to 26 Auborough St for treatment as it would be difficult to give it here. On his instructions I have examined every boy here this

evening and found no traces at all. They are mild cases and should be better in three or four days.

A. C. Goodwin

Two boys have had accidents. Coates injured his inner right arm on the Sports Field on Saturday morning. He was in hospital until yesterday afternoon and his arm has to be in plaster for another fortnight. Green slightly bruised his left arm, next the elbow, yesterday, in the gym. He is strapped up and has to see the doctor again on Friday.

A. C. Goodwin

[Re Norman Cooper]

I shall be glad if you will kindly arrange for the above boy to be referred to a private dental practitioner who would be willing to undertake such treatment in accordance with the scale fixed for dental treatment under the National Health Insurance Scheme. Under this scale a fee of 2/6d is payable for the extraction of each tooth up to three teeth. — (County Medical Officer)

Dear Dr Walker,

You will probably have heard that there is a case of scarlet fever at the Adelphi. The Medical Officer of Health has excluded all contacts with the boy (Hopkin) for ten days which means until the end of next week as he has already been in bed four days. IV alpha must also be excluded as they took lessons with that form. The boy has been taken to hospital and all precautions taken so we should be safe from an epidemic.

M. Sheppard

Dear Dr Walker,

We are managing quite well under difficulties. There are no more cases and all sore throats are immediately and rigorously dealt with. Almost the normal teaching periods are being done and we 'Adelphi four' pass from hotel to school like weavers' shuttles. We take the boys out for rapid walks as frequently as possible.

E. J. C. Large

Charles Taylor remembers the situation well. Scarlet fever was a serious matter in 1939 and the excluded children had to be kept away from all others. The long walks were taken whilst the others were in school and were enlivened by one humorist who would walk in front of the crocodile ringing a bell and calling out 'Unclean' whenever other people were near. From such small beginnings began the medical career of Dr Len Dean.

'Evacuadelphi' — We gargle
Think back! And surely there will climb
Up from the 'dark abysm of time'

> Those winter nights, when we lined up
> With salt and water in a cup,
> And gargled with effects symphonic,
> To stop sore throats from getting chronic.

The next letter is of interest in that it might be a clue as to what the children were expected to take with them for evacuation. It might also explain the letter that follows:

> Dear Son,
>
> I am coming on Saturday all being well so if you want to come home have all your things ready to put in the suit-case as there won't be a lot of time to spare.
>
> I haven't any more news to tell you but I am making you a list of what you have got there with you so that you can see if they are all there.
>
> National Registration Identity Card
> 2 towels   1 face cloth
> 6 shirts
> 4 vests
> 1 pr pants   2 suits
> football shorts, jersey, boots and socks
> 3 pairs socks
> 2 pair sandshoes
> 2 pair shoes
> 2 pair pyjamas
> brush, comb, scissors, tooth brush
> blazer
> 10 handkerchiefs
> scarf, raincoat
> mug, plate, knife, fork, spoons
> See you on Saturday,

[Note — no gas mask.]

> Dear Sir,
>
> I would be extremely grateful if you would consent to accept my son. I regret we had not the means to provide the boy with the necessary equipment at the time of the first evacuation.
>
> [The second paragraph is also of interest.]
>
> In the boy's own interest we must get him away if possible, he has nothing to occupy his time and consequently is bored and unhappy.

Homesickness inevitably became a serious problem. The staff worked hard to keep children occupied so that there would be little time for reflection. Few of these children would have ever been separated from their parents before, and the sudden upheaval, the phony war, and a gradual disenchantment with Scarborough in winter began to take its toll. Most parents expected some sort of trouble and encouraged their children to stay in Scarborough. Some were most punctilious about asking for permission to visit pupils whilst others responded to the first request and brought the child home.

On 14 September the *Hull Daily Mail* carried the heading, 'Mothers who are ruining Evacuation Scheme — children will settle if left alone.'

However, Kingston High School still had over 90% of its evacuees in mid-November 1939.

Parents' letters indicate some of the problems:

> Dear Miss Phillips,
> I am sorry to have to trouble you again but in her letter today she is quite homesick and is asking to be brought home.
>
> Your letter came as a shock but since you want so badly to come home I've given your fare to ... Also if you owe anything, ask for an account and I will send it next week, or part of it.
> Love from all,
> Mam

TELEGRAM 11.25 HULL 6 OCT 39
=COME HOME SATURDAY MORNING=DAD

> It appears by your last post card you would like to come home, well your Mam says you can do so.
> Pop

Dear Jim,
I have a surprise for you. Dad says you can come home so come on Saturday by bus. I have enclosed the fare... Never mind what anybody says. You come home...

I wish to bring him home. Most of his friends have returned and it has unsettled him, I don't think it wise to let him stay away when he is unhappy because I am quite sure he will not be doing justice to his school work when he is so depressed.

This is to inform you that I shall recall my son from Scarborough on Tuesday the 22nd October.

Dear Sir,
Just writing you these few lines on behalf of my son, staying at the Adelphi Hotel, to ask you if you will allow him to come home as I wish him to be at home here with me, now I am at home,

Photograph of boys outside the Adelphi Hotel, Scarborough.
Back row (left to right) Goodwin, Trip, Barker, Taylor, Wilkinson, Tate, Harbord, Finestein, Dean, Kersh, Vinegrad, Baker, Fitton, Hewitt, Wright, Scruton, Latus, Marshall.
Second row (left to right) Harper, Lill, Hopkins, Edmondson, Green, Plaxton, Crumpton, Watts W. G., Stanley, Coates, Gaudie, Hodgson, Oates, Williams, Hunter, Brabbs, Codd, Smith C. E., Fletcher, Ellerington, Smith H.
Front row (left to right) Potts, Bielby, Foyston, Smith R., Greenwood, Fraser, Miss Truefitt, Mrs Longstaff, Mr Goodwin, Mrs Goodwin, Mrs Truefitt, Mr Large, Mrs Scott, Mr Scott, Miss Carr, Mr Jordan, Harrison, Hemlin, Piercy, Longstaff J.

because every time he writes he is asking to come home and I am bad with my nerves and he will be able to help me with my little children and be company for me when his Dad is on nights.

I feel I have made a mistake in bringing him home but hope you will understand...

Will you please allow my son to come home by the 11.30 Thursday as we desire it, otherwise his Dad will come and fetch him...

TELEGRAM
=GO TO GRANNIES SON LOVE MAM +

A curious problem arose at that first Christmas. Children were used to finishing school and having a holiday. The teachers had a similar interest in the festive season. However, the Germans did not call a truce over the Christmas period and requests from parents, pupils or staff to leave the safe area and return to Hull were roundly condemned. The lack of any bombing over Hull and the lack of evident danger made the problem more acute. The Truefitts played their part in making Christmas better for the children by offering special rates for parents coming to Scarborough for Christmas.

Teachers were allowed to be away from Scarborough for up to 14 days with half the staff away from 15 December and the remainder from 29 December so that there would be adequate numbers for supervision. However, as the children had lost so much schooling at the commencement of the term, their holidays would be only from 22 December to 8 January which meant that, for part of the time the school was open, half the staff were absent, yet there was no complaint about the extra work load.

Cameron Walker wrote to the Hull Director of Education about pupils' Christmas holidays as early as 7 December. Parents were writing requests to him to withdraw their children for Christmas. Parents were given the official reply, that children should not be removed from Scarborough and that, if they did, accommodation would not be reserved for them should they return. The school made a private arrangement with the Scarborough billeting officer that allowed pupils to be away between 22 and 27 December only.

Dear Dr Walker,

Mrs Richardson, the landlady, has received an invitation to spend Christmas with relatives. If we knew definitely that all our boys would be staying here over Christmas she would be quite willing to refuse the invitation... Would it be right for me to tell the boys to ask their parents whether or not they will be called home for Christmas?

A. Wigglesworth

'Evacuadelphi' described Christmas as:
> We Feast
> Festive New Year and Christmas time,
> When tables, ranged on one long line
> Along the deserted hall,
> Creaked and groaned with loads of all
> The good things that the season brings.
>
> We sat enthroned like feasting kings,
> Had chicken, Christmas pudding, toasts
> In ginger wine, pies, fruit and hosts
> Of games, including 'Moving ghosts'.

'There were 30,000 school children in Hull and upwards of 500 school teachers on salary and not a child was receiving any educational service at all,' said the *Hull Daily Mail* on 10 November 1939. Shortly afterwards the schools in Hull were re-opened, firstly those on the outskirts, and then later the remainder just as soon as air raid shelters were ready.

Shelters at the new Kingston High building were a low priority as the building had never been occupied, and the school re-opened in Hull during November 1939 using the Newland High School premises for morning lessons only and with about half the staff brought back to Hull.

Cameron Walker reported later to parents:
> Miss Lee (Headmistress at Newland) will forgive me if I say that, at first, the appearance of trousers in the drive and corridors of Newland caused a certain amount of apprehension among the young ladies who normally occupy those premises, just as earlier, in Scarborough, our young ladies had produced some excitement amongst the boys of Scarborough High School. But presently shyness changed to curiosity, curiosity to mutual regard and finally regard to friendship. I am most happy to be able to say here that when, at last, we came to the Kingston High School on 11 March, a greetings telegram and flowers from our friends at Newland were here to welcome us. And I believe it is true to say also that the first social gathering to be held here was a tea-party given by our girl prefects to the prefects of Newland.

However, work started on building the shelters in January and authority to move pupils into their own building was given for 11 March 1940. There was a possibility of opening earlier, even earlier than the Grammar School in Leicester Street, but Cameron Walker wrote to his Head of Physics that he was prepared to delay opening so that the Grammar School would not be made to share the Kingston building with its fine new laboratories:
> For one thing I do not relish the idea of the Grammar School people using our apparatus in the absence of the Senior Science Master.

Once it was open, he wanted it all for his own school.

It was Frederick Cowell who was able to explain one section of the poem. He, with other boys, was on the front watching the tide come in and many of them were caught when an extra heavy wave took the boys by surprise. It seems to have taken the staff by surprise too, though there was a funny side to be seen later.

'Evacuadelphi' had:
> We are soaked
> Nor can your Lounge have seen the sight
> More strange than that one rainy night,
> When after dark, the firelight's gleaming
> Showed sixty pairs of trousers steaming
> As one ! black, brown, long, short and worn ones,
> Old, new, striped, spotty, patched and torn ones,
> Yes, sixty holey, rain-soaked pairs,
> Spread out on sixty backs of chairs!

While the pupils were enjoying their leisure time out of school, two members of staff were 'walking out'. This was a somewhat hazardous undertaking with several hundred pairs of eyes around. School pupils rarely realise that teachers are human and John Large and Marion Upex were able to keep their secret for quite a long time. Another looking forward to future marriage was a 6th-form pupil who was later to achieve renown as a Professor of Chemistry and to lecture at the Royal Institution, Charles A. Taylor. He was giving less time to science and more time in building up an acquaintanceship with Mrs Truefitt's daughter, an activity that also led to the altar.

Spare time activities included rather more than homework. Pupils tended to keep together rather than join Scarborough clubs and societies. The local library was popular and there is extant a letter requesting Frederick Cowell to return a book he borrowed and never returned while at Scarborough. The local vicar tried to encourage boys to join his confirmation classes but Cameron Walker required boys to have their parents' permission before joining. The staff contributed together to hire a piano for musical activities. As well as use by the choir, it provided support for dancing and community singing. Mr A.C. Goodwin was a keen dancer and regular sessions were held in one of the larger rooms. 'Ping Pong' had not yet graduated to 'Table Tennis' but nevertheless was a very popular pastime. The hotels supplied board games and there were charades, playlets, quizzes and competitions. Everything was done to keep all pupils active and not becoming homesick.

'Evacuadelphi':
> We Go High-Brow
> Wednesday nights at half past eight
> When we assembled to debate,
> Spell, answer questions: — 'Who is Venice?' —

Or watch the 'champs at table-tennis'
Control the rhythmic rise and fall
Of bat and celluloidal ball.

                    Night-Club
From half-past nine to half-past ten,
The Rec came to its own again,
When Tate, Kersh, Harbord and the rest
Smashed chairs and ping-pong balls with zest;
While the jazz-fiend of the party,
Going high-brow and Mozarty,
Played with tinkle, trill and boom,
'An 18th-century Drawing Room'.

                    Devilry in the Dining-Room
Impromptu dances late at night,
To Mr Goodwin's great delight.
Wilkinson moving stiffly through
The steps of dances old and new;
Baker's fox-trotting impression,
Done with the proper bored expression;
See him waltzing, debonair,
With his supercilious air;
Up and down the room he goes
Mainly on Mrs Longstaff's toes.

Dean curvetting, Taylor striding
Half the hall's length; all colliding
With the chairs, and when they're able
Stumbling round the billiard-table.
Kersh at billiards, Grimwood twiddling
Wireless knobs in lieu of fiddling.

The children were very well looked after throughout the Scarborough stay but there will always be complaints and some parents listened to every rumour going round. One hotel received very bad publicity and pupils were withdrawn to Hull on that basis alone. One parent wrote:
> I visited the hotel three weeks ago and was not impressed with the comfort of the place which leaves room for a good deal of improvement. The food should certainly be better.

In reply Cameron Walker sent a day's menu and information about the accommodation:

                    Wednesday 1st November —

Breakfast   Baked beans on toast
                     Bread and butter *ad lib*
                     Tea; marmalade

Dinner	Steak and kidney pie
	Potatoes *ad lib*
	Rice pudding
Tea (Tuesday)	1 crumpet
	Bread and butter
	Jam, cake, tea
Supper	Cocoa, bread and butter

Bedroom — your son shares one of the front bedrooms with two other boys. The management have no further supplies of blankets and I suggested that each boy, when he went home for a week-end, should bring back a blanket which he could take home with him when he left. Your son has not done this although one of the others has brought his.

I am aware that at first the food was not satisfactory at this hotel but I made representations and matters were rectified quickly. Several boys from that billet today told me that the food was now good. I fail to see how anyone could make better provision than the above on 8/6d a week; nor do I think any more than the above is necessary.

Another parent wrote:
    I am writing about my daughter at Scarborough. When she was at the Forsyte she was fairly comfortable but this new billet seems a terrible place. According to her letter, they get porridge for breakfast which they can't eat, (does not remember dinner) but for tea only a LITTLE bread and a LITTLE jam and no mention of any supper. She says each girl has to send home each week for a parcel of food, only cold water to use, and practically no fire, as she says, one shovelful in six hours. The beds are damp and they have to turn them each night. One girl who has no blanket of her own has to be content with one blanket and no sheet even. They are never warm. Under these circumstances I am going to bring her home.

Cameron Walker replied fully to this letter:
    Very early in September I had a complaint that the food was not ample enough for our big girls and I understood that the matter had been remedied. It has been one of the most satisfactory billets we have had and the fact that the number of girls there has remained constant goes to show that the billet is satisfactory. I understand that they provide sheets and one blanket, the girls were asked to provide extra blankets from home and all the girls have done this.
    If I were you I should be careful about saying that the beds are damp. It is a punishable offence for boarding house keepers to put

people into damp beds and I am quite certain that the hotel would take suitable action. It is certainly not true.

Your daughter may attend at the Newland High School on Monday next at 8.25 am.

The lack of any servant provision in the large hotel billets meant that everyone had to take part in domestic work. Staff and pupils undertook all duties and that even included rising early to light fires, warm water and prepare breakfasts. Miss Phillips got rid of table cloths at the Astoria so that there was less to keep clean. When she was in charge there she occupied a large bedroom to herself which had a dressing table that was covered with bottles of pills and lotions. This grand collection was for the girls, and every day she held 'surgery', giving out whatever prescription belonged to a girl. Miss Phillips became expert at putting drops in eyes and ears, and in dealing with first aid problems. As there was never any hot water in the mornings until the fires were lit, the mistresses were in the habit of filling a hot water bottle before going to bed, and this tepid liquid was used for washing the next morning. The girls used cold water. Mrs Large (then Miss Upex) remembers stamping hard on the bread room floor in the dark on a winter's morning to frighten away any mice before she ventured to put on the light and start to cut and butter the bread for 130 hungry girls.

Everything has to come to an end and the evacuation to Scarborough ended in the autumn of 1940. The Battle of Britain and the fall of France were the deciding factors in moving children from Scarborough. Right from the start some parents had considered it an unsafe place for the evacuation of children. A second party left Hull in July 1940 for Bourne in Lincolnshire where for a few months happy relationships were built up with Bourne Grammar School and the local community. However, having sections of the school at Bourne, Hull and Scarborough was inefficient and plans were laid to take the two evacuated sections to Bingley in the West Riding, where both parties met up during September 1940, happily taking with them not just the staff, pupils, masses of luggage and school materials but also scabies.

The Evacuees at Bingley, October 1940

The Valiant Three Hundred

A List of Evacuees made 16 October 1939

Billet 1, 27 Grosvenor Crescent
(IV alpha)

Betty Blanshard	Mary Pretty	Barbara Robinson
Mary Willmot	Joan Wray	Margaret Morris
Margery Carter	Elsie Bell	Lois Rogers
Dorothy Dick	Joyce Hayton	Pauline Dalton
Jean Farrington	Peggy Shepherdson	Audrey Greenhead
Barbara Oxtoby	Kathleen Roberts	Edith Raine
Dorothy Moore		

Billet 2, Doris Court, Albion Road
(VI beta)

Audrey Avis	Marjorie Berry	Edna Carr
Rosabel Doonan	Enid Featherstone	Valerie Hickman
Sheila Middlebrook	Dorothy Owen	Eileen Smithson
Joan Stokoe	Kathleen Train	Molly Ward
Mary Fenwick	Joyce Carmichael	

Billet 3, Prince of Wales Hotel
(IIa, IIb)

Arthur Anderson	Malcolm Collinson	Roy Cornthwaite
Alfred Hancock	Robert Hawes	Thomas Jefferson
William Kneeshaw	Anthony Lister	Edward McNeil
Paul Middleton	George Padmore	John Pitts
Ernest Richardson	Colin Shakespeare	Gordon Suddaby
D. Taylor	John Watson	L. Wells
Leonard White	Dennis Winsor	Norman Woollven

Kenneth Andrews	Charles Atkinson	Arnold Brooks
John Farrow	Dennis Fewster	Norman Harrison
Leslie Harrison	Eric Hemlin	Ronald Mountain
Ernest Roustoby	George Sanders	Gerald Staveley
Frank Stevenson	Alan Woodhall	Geoffrey Dukes
Dennis Piercey		

Billet 4, Windsor Hotel
(IIIa)

Kenneth Barnes	Eric Bentley	Richard Brocklebank
Edgar Cross	Stanley Dobbs	Trevor Ellerington

Richard Fraser   Kenneth Fletcher   Stanley Gibbs
Colin Hotham   James Jolley   Kenneth Louis
George Mitchell   Frank Seaman   Ernest Squire
Kenneth Tilley   Leslie Bryan   Norman Summersgill
Sydney Chambers

Billet 5, Grafton House, 32 Esplanade Gardens
(V alpha)

Daphne Agar   Nancy Beall   Mary Bousfield
Joan Dinning   Joan Dobson   Joan Finch
Margaret Hanby   Joyce Holland   Barbara Medforth
Evelyn Mitchell   Joan Norris   Joan Parker
Eileen Robinson   Marjory Saynor   Betty Whitelam
Audrey Spurr

Billet 6, 22 Esplanade Gardens
(V beta)

Joan Atkinson   Audrey Dexter   Mary Johnson
Barbara Kemp   Marjorie Thompson

Billet 7, Adelphi Hotel Esplanade (previously at 20 Esplanade Gardens)
(Vb)

Peter Gaudie   Anthony Fitton   Ronald Lill
Alexander Owen   Walter Peskey   Roland Williams
G. Coates   Kenneth Thompson   Leonard Hewitt
Bruce Cawthorne   Ronald Cook   William Oates

Billet 8, Holbeck Private Hotel, Esplanade (previously at 14 Esplanade Gardens)

Terence Ellerington Gordon Fenwick   Norman Cooper
Ernest Cowell   Frederick Cowell   Leslie Fish
Dennis Holmes   Arthur Jones   John Joy
John Moss   Raymond Styles

Billet 9, 43 Esplanade Road

Donald Ash   Kenneth Reynolds   J. Bielby
Clifford Coates   Colin Ansell   Peter Brainbridge
Dennis Cowton   Stuart Crumpton   William Knight
Maurice Nelmes   Alan Plaxton   Charles Potts
Harry Stanley   Ernest Westoby   Joseph Adams

Billet 10, Forsyte Private Hotel, Esplanade Road
VI beta)

Joan Atkinson	Moira Nelmes	Mavis Holey
Marjorie Barnes	Gladys Brown	Cecile Cooper
Joan Dowson	Cora Duguid	Kathleen Goldspink
Madonna Squire	Marjorie Mault	

Billet 11, Holbeck Private Hotel, Esplanade (previously at 5 Granville Road)

L. Hardwick	Joseph Key	Donald Pell
Sidney Pidd	John Pinder	Robert Smith
William Tipple	Norman Towell	Peter Walton
William Wilkinson	Brian Willis	

Billet 12, Astoria Hotel

Betty Blackbourne	Doreen Bellamy	Lily Brown
Winifred Fish	Eileen Harrison	Joyce Holdsworth
Audrey Hole	Betty Kent	Eileen Marshall
Alice Pedder	Geraldine Rodgers	Margaret Russell
Brenda Ayre	Mary Barron	Mary Byers
Janette Cousins	Anita Gerstein	Joyce Hams
Mary Hood	Vera Hood	Joan Longley
Ivy Longley	Rita Silkovitz	Ethwyn Stephens
Mavis Townend		
Audrey Clarke	Doreen Cook	Barbara Cranswick
Alice Davison	Pauline Elliott	Freda Gerstein
Joyce Hemsworth	Marjorie Mason	Rita Newiss
Eileen Nicholson	Clarice Orvis	Joan Robinson
Jacqueline Turner	Marjorie Whitehead	Jean Willman
Shirley Steer		
Doreen Bates	Mavis Brown	Joan Curtis
Joan Dean	Dorothy Elliott	Mary Frank
Monica Gibson	Eileen Graystone	Jean Hughes
Olga Jones	Joan Keal	Kathleen Lawty
Monica Oxtoby	Betty Pickering	Mary Potts
Betty Richardson		
Alice Betts	Dorothy Salmond	Joyce Edmond
Nellie Soulsby	Joyce Williams	Muriel Wells
Audrey Brown	Audrey Atkinson	Stella Black

Doreen Brook	Anita Chapman	Kathleen Collier
Marie Cooper	Elizabeth Fawcett	Catherine Hood
Sheila Kearns	Audrey Lumb	Joyce Mills
Jean Rhodes	Patricia Best	Enid Saynor
Rosemary Ellyard	Ann Sugarman	Margaret Hargreaves
Pamela Berriman	June Fitches	Pauline Fletcher
Sheila Kingston	Jean Leighton	Patricia Lynch
Ivy Marshall	Sheila Matson	Thelma Medforth
Irene Robinson	Betty Sellers	Doreen Watts
Barbara Whiting	Lilias Woollven	Dorothy Young
Mary Young	Berenice Harrison	Eva Cornick

Billet 13, Adelphi Hotel

David Edmondson	D. Foyston	Noel French
Geoffrey Greenwood	Harry Harper	Denis Hopkin
David Mitchell	Alan Pool	Henry Smith
Raymond Smith	Alan Green	David Wilson

Albert Abbott	John Baker	Alan Bonner
Albert Brabbs	Cyril Codd	Clifford Farrar
Peter Hodgson	Norman Hunter	Henry Kemmenoe
Harold Kersh	Anthony Kidson	George Knapton
Norman Latus	Frank Marshall	Ernest May
Alan Scruton	Charles Smith	James Thorley
Ronald Watts	Peter Wright	Gordon Smith

Peter Benstead	Anthony Fitton	Frank Forster
Roland Williams	Israel Finestein	John Barker
Norman Tate	Charles Taylor	Henry Trip
Len Dean	Thomas Mirfin	Gordon Wilkinson
William Harbord	Peter Grimwood	Leon Vinegrad
James Gettings	R. Goodwin	

HULL EVACUATION SCHEME

Please PASS

Name ....

Address ....

Assembly Point ....

Signed ....
                                             Leader or Helper